Monetary Women's Activist:
A Cutting edge Lady's Manual for a Well off Life

By

Karen W. Day

Table of Content:

Introduction

What Is Monetary Women's liberation?

For a really long time, ladies have had the monetary chances stacked against them, and 2021 was the same: orderly mistreatment, orientation generalizations, and absence of schooling (among numerous different variables!) have driven ladies to bring in and set aside less money. This puts single ladies, divorced ladies and LGBTQ ladies in a difficult situation, and adds one more layer of trouble for wedded ladies in miserable or oppressive unions with leave.

Monetary woman's rights are tied in with assuming back command over your funds, developing a monetary establishment, and taking space in the monetary world so you can carry on with the existence you need now and into retirement.

The objective is to accomplish independence from the rat race, which offers ladies the chance to make their own choices with the cash they've acquired. Would you like to have a kid? Could you like to venture to the far corners of the planet for a very long time? With independence from the rat race, you can pursue these choices without being subject to another person's cash.

Chapter One

The Feelings Of Cash:

There are a lot of feelings joined to cash since cash is so effectively used to pass judgment on others. By being interested in which feeling we're feeling and dialing back our dynamic cycle, we can pursue more proactive monetary choices that will assist us with living all the more deliberately. Cash is personal and isn't generally tackled with a number cruncher. There are a ton of feelings connected to cash since cash is so effortlessly used to pass judgment on others. By being interested in which feeling we're feeling and dialing back our dynamic cycle, we can pursue more proactive monetary choices that will assist us with living all the more purposefully. Something simple alludes to the fact that it is so hard to really do. Sadly, individual budget is difficult. Cash isn't a numerical question; cash is a brain research issue. It's tied in with dealing with our feelings and our ways of behaving. That is difficult to educate, learn, and execute. You can consider individual accounting as having different sides. The primary side is the outside side. This is what the majority of us think about when we think about cash. There are the mechanics, procedures, and strategies that we attempt to execute. Outside finance is where you track down the math. The opposite side is the inside side of cash. Inside finance is where we track down our feelings, sentiments, and inspiration. All the outside monetary information on the planet won't help us assuming we can't or are reluctant to execute that information. The main thing to acknowledge in the wake of learning cash is personal is that cash is hard for everyone. There are a ton of pessimistic feelings joined to cash, including culpability, disgrace, envy, tension, dread, and lament. You've known about a portion of these ideas previously, yet maybe perhaps not in the setting. Envy is the main thrust behind our endeavors to stay aware of the Joneses.

These and numerous different feelings are attached to our monetary ways of behaving as a whole and choices. We will do a great deal to stay away from gloomy feelings. One counteractant to figuring out how to more readily acknowledge gloomy feelings is care. At the point when we figure out how to acknowledge our feelings without judgment, we can all the more likely oversee them. A large portion of how we manage our cash looks bad to an external eyewitness. Notwithstanding, assuming you comprehend the profound condition of the individual settling on the choice or the Cash Content that is driving these choices, each choice seems OK.

Individual budget Essentials ARE Straightforward.

It's not difficult to accept that individual budgets and contributions are just numerical questions. We feel that on the grounds that the rudiments are basic. The fundamentals incorporate spending short of what you make, putting something aside for the future, and not committing any enormous errors. Due to this apparent effortlessness, we accept in the event that we just had more data, a superior condition, or more information, we would pursue better monetary choices. Then we are difficult for ourselves when we don't accomplish what we set off to do. We could try and uncertainty our knowledge since we were unable to sort out the numerical question. Since something is basic doesn't mean it's simple.

A distinction between something is being straightforward and something simple. A few things can be both basic and simple, such as taking care of your lawn. A few things are neither basic nor simple, similar to advanced science, for instance.

Effortlessness is about ideas and rules. Something contrary to effortlessness is intricacy. Simple is about a low degree of trouble. Something contrary to simple is hard, or troublesome.

Individual accounting and putting fall into the camp of basic on these grounds that the ideas are really clear.

Cash doesn't fall into the camp of simple, notwithstanding, in light of the fact that cash is close to home.

Practice Monetary Self-empathy

self-empathy can be characterized as stretching out the elegance to yourself utilizing three components: self-consideration, normal mankind, and care. Normal mankind is the possibility that the "human experience is blemished, that we are unsteady" — that will be, that defects, mix-ups, and dissatisfaction are widespread — and care is a "nonjudgmental, open brain state" where you notice your contemplations and sentiments with interest.

Monetary self-sympathy, then, at that point, is the capacity to perceive that we as a whole commit monetary errors and that is fine. Dissimilar to individual accounting exhortation that rebukes people for screwing up, rehearsing monetary self-sympathy can assist people with being more straightforward about themselves.

To perceive how monetary self-sympathy functions by and by, envision you were late on a Visa bill. You could utilize monetary self-sympathy by first rehearsing some care. Taking a couple of rounds of full breaths, you could stretch out graciousness and normal mankind to yourself by saying, "While it's not great, it's likewise not the apocalypse that I missed the due date on that Visa bill. We aren't shown this in school, and a great deal of the language is befuddling and overpowering. I'm in good company to bring in a cash botch."

Whenever you've drilled monetary self-empathy, make all the difference for the forward movement. Put that Visa bill on autopay, and set an update on your schedule to look at your financial record something like one time per month.

Try not to allow disgrace to prevent you from requesting help

Cash disgrace happens when we commit an error and let ourselves know that we are terrible individuals in view of the blunder. It very well may be particularly extreme since individuals will generally keep such a great deal of their monetary lives private. Without a trace of open discussions, individuals will generally expect that others are savvier than they are, and judge themselves for not improving monetarily. Quite possibly the most widely recognized opinion I hear as a monetary specialist is, "The manner by which ds every other person understands how to manage their cash yet me?" When we experience monetary disgrace, it can make it hard to request help, find out about cash, or do whatever it takes to work on monetary prosperity. Scientist and other creators has found four things that assist with mitigating disgrace:

- Individual weakness,
- Basic mindfulness,
- Connecting,
- And talking disgrace.

In my work, I've found committing the significance of the error, social help, and marking the individual weakness to be strong strides toward taking out cash disgrace.

There are numerous ways you can request monetary assistance. You can begin with free assets, such as paying attention to web recordings about cash or looking at some individual accounting books from the library. In the event that perusing and listening isn't sufficient, and you're as yet uncertain about how you really want to manage your individual accounting records, you could ponder taking a free or minimal-expense online course. Online courses cover all that from planning to credit reimbursement to money management.

At long last, on the off chance that you want more monetary expert direction and hand-holding, consider finding a charge-just monetary organizer who has experience assisting individuals with the close-to-home side of cash. A monetary specialist can be a decent choice, as well.

Praise your cash wins

In my monetary treatment work, I welcome clients to share occurrences where they were "great" with cash, and they frequently surrender models like putting something aside for an excursion, opening up a retirement account, or settling a charge card. Whenever I've paid attention to what they've done, I request that they share sentiments related to those positive monetary activities; I've heard answers like "quiet, glad, strong, energized." When you are dealing with making a sound connection with cash, remember to respite and give yourself credit.

Since encountering cash disgrace frequently mists our capacity to praise the times when we've gone with positive decisions, I suggest that all individuals dealing with a monetary arrangement incorporate little ways of expenditure the cash that will give them real pleasure and permit them to invest heavily in their successes. Perhaps you don't get the latte consistently, however, you indulge yourself with one week after a week. Or on the other hand on the off chance that you are dealing with putting something aside for an initial installment.

It is strong to Celebrate monetary achievement. At the point when we commend our advancement en route, it builds up that we are equipped for working on our relationship with cash. Research has found that the more habitually we experience a feeling of progress, similar to a "little win," the more probable we are to proceed with that good way of behaving. Also, with regard to funds? The more we commend those sorts of wins, the more it affirms that we can be in every way great with cash.

How feelings assume a part in dealing with your cash

While cash isn't all that matters, keeping reserve funds and enjoying them in accordance with your individual monetary goals is significant. Contingent upon your ongoing circumstance and long-haul plans, you will need to deal with your cash diversely at different times all throughout your life.

It's a well-known fact that cash and feeling remain closely connected. We strive to deal with our families, deal with ourselves, and set something aside for the future, so it's nothing unexpected that cash is a personal point for a great many people. Cash can influence our feelings of anxiety, psychological well-being, and individual connections.

To more readily isolate your feelings from your cash, we've made four moves to assist you with ending up being more certain and less worried about your monetary future.

1. Begin with a financial plan

Quite possibly the earliest move toward dealing with your cash - and the feelings encompassing it - is to make a financial plan. A spending plan can assist with removing a portion of the pressure cash makes since it gives you an activity plan. Explicitly stating your financial plan can assist you with a better comprehension of how much cash is coming in and leaving your family, and all the more critically, what the cash is being spent on every month.

This information and association can assist with cutting superfluous buys and making a drawn-out investment funds plan. It ought to likewise be a functioning report that you and everybody in your family survey and examine together consistently.

2. Settle in being awkward

A spending plan isn't an end-all, be-all answer for cash for the executives. Life can toss you curves, and at times change can be hard. Another kid, school, separation, retirement and, surprisingly, clinical occasions can leave you feeling overpowered sincerely and monetarily.

In these awkward times, it's vital to address what is happening head-on and track down a drawn-out arrangement that works for your loved ones. Frequently, the most ideal way to figure out these circumstances is to talk with somebody about your interests and work together to track down the most ideal way to push ahead monetarily. It's OK to request help from a companion, broker, or confided-in relative.

3. Clarify some pressing issues and figure out your funds

In the event that you're not associated with your family's funds, one simple method for learning more is to request that your accomplice show you your family spending plan and your ongoing monetary circumstance. It's to be expected for individuals to play an optional job with regards to dealing with their family's funds if their companion or critical different has started to lead the pack. However, the two individuals actually must know where their cash is coming in and where it's going out every month.

To make the way for a real to life discussion about cash, begin by showing revenue in the family funds and make yourself accessible to talk.

4. Check in and update your objectives

In the event that you are now on a strong monetary way or on the other hand on the off chance that you are simply starting, it is consistently smart to meet with your financier or track down a confided-in monetary counselor. A broker can ensure that you are in good shape, whether that is dealing with your obligation, adjusting your financial plan, putting something aside for a major occasion, or preparing for retirement. They can assist with surveying your spending plan and monetary guide and update as fundamental so your feelings are more reasonable when huge life-altering situations occur.

At the point when you search out a financier or monetary counsel, make certain to see whether they are a trustee. A guardian is legitimately committed to figuring out your greatest advantage and searching for what makes a difference to you, not what is important to themselves or to the monetary establishment where they work. Making time to have a discussion with an investor or monetary guide to comprehend your funds is basic to deal with your feelings about cash. Don't hesitate for even a moment to seek clarification on some things - learning is the initial step to turning out to be monetarily sure.

You merit certifiable help from a confidential financier who's set up their sleeves for you. We are here with you bit by bit to plan, conceptualize and deal with your particular monetary necessities. Figure out more about our Confidential Bank and interface with a confidential financier.

Impacts Of Cash On Your Feelings

There is no culture on Earth that has found cash and afterward chose not to utilize it... Cash is a valuable device to work with human association and progression,

Cash holds an extremely strong influence over a singular's feelings, character, and choices. Furthermore, it can impact the choices of small kids more than we understand.

"In the circumstance that I desired a lifting of hands on those who like the wealthy, I don't anticipate seeing a lot of hands go up in the room. Short of what 33% of grown-ups say they like the rich.

In any case, youngsters answer in an unexpected way, There has been a ton of examination that kids as youthful as 4 years of age show inclination for those with more noteworthy riches. So what occurs as we age? One clarification is that kids' mentalities are at the verifiable level, and grown-ups are at the express level.

At the express level, members predominantly favored the working class over poor people, and people the working class over the rich. Be that as it may, at the understood level, members favored the rich over the working class.

So then, at that point, what is people's opinion about the abundance they have?

Abrupt abundance condition is distinguished as extreme culpability for something an individual doesn't really accept that they're qualified for. The possibility of abundance responsibility is a distinct difference from the general generalizations of rich people, where abundance causes an expansion in privilege and deservingness. Be that as it may, on the off chance that a singular feels they are not qualified for something, frequently they feel culpability for anything it is they gotten.

Abundance responsibility doesn't correspond with how much cash the individual has, and isn't related to orientation or identity. It is exactly unmistakable from different kinds of responsibility.

Does cash make us less liberal?

There are two unique modes we will generally work in,

- common mode: Focuses on helping somebody without requiring reimbursement;

we benefit others to show concern, typically toward family and dear companions. Mutual mode is distinguished by specific ways of behaving, like aiding and liberality.

- Market mode: We are in a business exchange. We are offering or tolerating an advantage with the assumption for tantamount return, Market mode is more common in a business relationship.

The scientists are estimated to support a collective way of behaving and task execution as market conduct. As per the scientists, initiating one mode ought to deliver ways of behaving predictably with it and impede incongruent ways of behaving.

Youngsters helped to remember cash, contrasted with different items, were less liberal to peers; were less useful; all the more frequently disregarded specialists' solicitations; and took more rewards. They likewise worked longer and harder and were more fruitful at troublesome errands. The examples seen by the scientists reproduce those of grown-ups' and uncover that youngsters begin to learn market ways of behaving
since the beginning.

Step-by-step instructions to Be Genuinely Offset With Cash

Could it be said that you are genuinely adjusted with regard to cash? Indeed, you realize you want to save, financial plan, take care of obligations, and plan for retirement, yet how would you feel with regards to your funds?

It's not difficult to discuss how we ought to do our cash without truly zeroing in on the profound viewpoint. We frequently deal with cash like numerous different things throughout everyday life — a necessary evil.

Nonetheless, cash gigantically affects how individuals get to carry on with their lives. Furthermore, therefore, it's regular that we will generally connect a lot of feeling to it. Here and there these feelings can be pessimistic which can prompt more pressing issues for example profound spending, venturing into the red, and so on.

Yet, before we jump into how to adjust feelings around cash, we should examine what pessimistic feelings about your funds can mean for you.

The impacts of not being genuinely offset with cash

Having cash blocks, depending on profound thinking, and not being sincerely adjusted can adversely affect your psychological well-being. Assuming your monetary circumstance has you intemperament, know that you're in good company.

Northwestern Common's Preparation and Progress Investigation discovered that while 68% of Americans felt better about their monetary circumstance, a significant measure of individuals likewise detailed feeling these pessimistic feelings routinely:

- Tension: 54%
- Monetary weakness: 52%
- Dread: 48%

Cash is likewise the predominant wellspring of stress, more than individual connections and having some work or vocation. In any case, monetary pressure can come to fruition in alternate ways, as well. It can likewise make individuals foster aversion ways of behaving with regard to their funds.

Monetary refusal is a guard system that might accompany sensations of dishonor and low confidence. If neglected, this can hold you back from accomplishing your monetary objectives or more regrettable.

In this way, figuring out how to adjust feelings with regard to cash is crucial for monetary achievement!

Rundown of pessimistic feelings around cash and turning out to be genuinely adjusted

Assuming that you're feeling tension, disgrace, or other gloomy feelings, perhaps now is the ideal time to investigate what's happening and set those sentiments straight. Here is a rundown of gloomy feelings around cash, alongside strategies to assist you with tracking down your balance.

- **Nervousness and dread**

Nervousness and dread are at the first spot on the list of gloomy feelings. Having nervousness or a feeling of dread toward cash is really quite normal.

Keep in mind, the greater part of Americans have a restless outlook on their cash consistently! You realize your internal discourse best. Perhaps you stress over how you'll procure enough of it and how you'll take care of your bills.

Or on the other hand, maybe you stress that you'll lose what you have or that you can't oversee it all alright. You stress such a great amount over your monetary circumstance that it becomes distressing and you stay away from your funds by and large.

Step-by-step instructions to get genuinely adjusted with regard to fear

Balance feelings of dread by escaping your own particular manner. When you begin regretting your cash, rather than remaining stuck, ask yourself, How might I move beyond this? On the off chance that you stress over not having the option to cover your bills, work with what you have some control over and make an arrangement.

Stressed over neglecting to cover your bills? Computerize your funds. In the event that you're pondering where all your cash is going consistently, make a spending plan and put forth monetary objectives.

In the event that it's all excessively overpowering, converse with a responsibility accomplice or cash master, or consider taking one of our free individual budget courses. Try not to permit yourself to remain stuck. Make a move one offsetting feeling with cash so you can work past the trepidation.

Outrage and lament

These are the shoulda, woulda, and coulda feelings. Perhaps you're irate with yourself for going to a shopping gorge or not setting aside sufficient cash. Perhaps you have lamented about opening that charge card and piling up unpaid liability.

You clutch such a lot of disappointment. And afterward, there's the outrage. Maybe you blow up at yourself for being so reckless.

Or then again perhaps you lash out at your folks for not showing you cash. In any case, you can gain from your monetary mix-ups and improve.

Instructions to adjust feelings of outrage

Anyway, how would you get sincerely adjusted assuming you feel outraged and lament? Rather than lament, think of pardoning. Excuse yourself for your past monetary errors and keep it moving. Heard the adage, "There's no utilization worrying over nothing?" All things considered, there's no reason to lament since it wastes your time.

It's alright to fly off the handle, yet channel those furious sentiments into great use. Blow up that your outlook becomes one of "at absolutely no point in the future."

Lash out that you make a strong spending plan and technique that guarantees you never fall once more into your approaches to inadequately dealing with your funds. Try not to clutch lament and outrage. Let them out, let them go, and continue to push ahead.

Disgrace and humiliation

With regard to cash, errors, disgrace, and shame are excessively normal. Perhaps you feel disgraced since you feel individuals will pass judgment on you for your cash botches. Or then again you have a humiliated outlook on your ongoing monetary circumstance.

We need to great search before our loved ones. We would rather not concede our cash circumstance isn't excessively perfect, particularly when society is letting us know that we ought to get specific things done monetarily by a specific age.

Fortunately, everybody has committed errors, even the most brilliant and richest individuals on the planet, and accept me when I say they've made a few.

Simply do a Google search on your #1 effective individuals. Any individual who lets you know they've never made a mix-up with their cash simply hasn't made one yet.

Get sincerely adjusted with regard to the disgrace

Like displeasure and lament, the way to adjust feelings from disgrace is to pardon yourself for your past cash missteps and afterward acknowledge you have nothing to demonstrate to anybody except for yourself.

Now is the right time to relinquish the disgrace and self-judgment and on second thought track down your inward solidarity to take the illustrations you've learned and push ahead.

Envy

The grass generally looks greener on the opposite side until you get to the opposite side and acknowledge things aren't what they appear. Desire likewise arrives in a milder structure known as "staying aware of the Joneses."

Step-by-step instructions to get genuinely offset by supplanting envy with appreciation

The way to adjust feelings around desire is to rehearse appreciation and satisfaction all things being equal. Get some downtime consistently to help yourself to remember the things you needed in the past that you currently have. Begin an appreciation diary or rundown, or download an application.

Free yourself of envy, and on second thought channel those sentiments into inspiration to work harder, tweak your monetary objectives, and improve inside your means. What's more, consistently recall, there are things you have that another person is petitioning God for.

Get genuinely offset with cash!

Do you connect with something from this rundown of pessimistic feelings? It's human instinct to feel pessimistic feelings, however, what is important is that you make a move and begin adjusting feelings that relate to your funds.

Chapter Two:

The Monetary Approaches

What is the monetary blueprint?

The monetary strategy includes determining monetary objectives including the sending, funding, and contributing plans expected to arrive at the objectives

A decent monetary arrangement resembles an outline for a manufacturer.

An arrangement ought to illuminate each part of how to gather and develop riches and accommodate crises.

Moves toward Your Monetary Strategies

Have you given any thought to what your monetary strategy is? Have you distinguished what your monetary objectives are? Your monetary strategy ought to incorporate a survey of your resources and obligations, a conversation of your monetary objectives, and activity moves toward getting you rolling in the correct bearing.

Your monetary objectives will assist you with making your arrangement for the following five to a decade. You ought to conclude whether you might want to claim a house or whether you would like to lease. At the point when you intend to claim a house, you should anticipate an initial installment, which ought to be roughly 20% of the price tag of the home. This implies for a $200,000 home, you ought to have $40,000 set aside. You will likewise require a little money or credit for home redesigns and, surprisingly, corrective things, like new paint, another back-sprinkle in the kitchen, or new fixtures. On the off chance that your monetary objective is to lease a home, you ought to likewise decide whether there will be a month-to-month affiliation charge or some other related costs with leasing the home. These charges could incorporate a

support charge, a vermin control expense, or a stopping expense.

Activity steps are essential to keep you moving in the correct course. You ought to likewise survey these activity steps every three or four months to ensure you are dealing with them and proceeding to push ahead. You ought to likewise survey the means and decide whether anything should be changed because of an adjustment of the situation - a new obligation, a kid, or some other situation. Coming up next are some move steps you can initiate to push toward your monetary objectives:

- **Audit your rundown of resources and obligations and choose how to settle obligations:** On the off chance that your base regularly scheduled installments are preposterously high, you might have to think about chapter 11 as a choice. In the event that you can square away your obligation, you need to pay however much you can to settle your obligation every single month.

- **Make a spending plan**: Ensure your spending plan incorporates your costs, regardless of whether they are all month to month. Incorporate your vehicle protection, pet supplies, veterinary consideration, and day camp costs. Choose where you need to spend your cash and choose who might want to spend your cash. The sooner you can square away your obligation, the sooner you can begin setting more cash aside for your fantasies and other monetary objectives.

- **Make an investment funds plan**: A decent rule of theirs is to put 10% of every check into an investment account. In the event that you get rewards, extra time pay, or an expense discount, attempt and store the cash to the side without contacting it. This will assist you with making a backup stash for costs, for example, a vehicle fix, a home fix, or a health-related crisis. Life will constantly have a startling occasions. Plan appropriately.

- **Minimize your costs**: On the off chance that you want to take care of your home loan in five years, you will most likely be unable to get another vehicle like clockwork. Focus on what is significant and keep your other costs low. This doesn't imply that you can't feast out three times each week, yet perhaps you can provide an uplink to minimize your costs. I live in Florida and cooling is non-debatable. For my purposes, that implies I probably won't feast at cafés as frequently throughout the mid-year in light of the fact that my electric bill will be higher. Utilizing the barbecue is a special reward!

- **Put yourself positioned for an extraordinary FICO rating:** Incredible acknowledgment can assist you to lower fascinating rates on home loans and vehicle credits. Extraordinary credit can assist you with opening up another Mastercard if there should be an occurrence of a crisis cost. A lawyer companion of mine had the two of his and his significant other's vehicles added up during Typhoon Irma. On account of his incredible credit, he had the option to fund two vehicles before the protection checks showed up. At the point when the protection checks show up and are utilized to settle the more current vehicle acquisitions, he will move his marvelous credit along.

- **Incorporate a critical other when everything looks good:** No one but you can know when the ideal opportunity to integrate a huge other into your monetary objectives is. A decent guideline is that a discussion about monetary objectives ought to happen before a wedding. It ought to likewise happen before you open a shared service or cover bills together. Great correspondence and a joint arrangement will positively help a relationship.

- **Be available to switch around your arrangement:** Life will adjust your course at least a couple of times. Be available for the change. Audit your monetary course of action and conclude what necessities to change. Do you have to diminish saving to address another cost? Could you at any point build the sum you pay towards your home loan consistently in view of an advancement? Do you have to cut costs in view of hospitalization? Adjusting your monetary course of action to your ongoing requirements is significant.

Monetary Arranging Interaction

The right speculation methodology and sound monetary exhortation will decide how you live today and later on. There are six phases to fostering a monetary arrangement and doing individual cash for the executives. From start to finish, a confirmed monetary organizer proficiently aids you through the monetary arranging process - keeping in view what is going on and the financial foundation.

1) Distinguish What is going on

The primary phase of the monetary arranging process is the evaluation of what's going on in your life at the present time and how you can change what is happening. The vital regions to reflect on are:

Family planning - This is a significant region as subsequent to working out the month-to-month costs spent at home, you'd have the option to sort out the amount you are left with to save or contribute.

Family responsibilities and Everyday costs - Would you say you are single or hitched? Do you have kids? What are their living and way of life costs?

Charge Standing and Techniques - How would you oversee charges? Is it true that you are living or working abroad?

Current ventures or saving stores - How much investment funds or obligations do you have at this moment?

Other Monetary commitments - These may include a few random costs you may be preparing for the future, for example,

• A wedding or property buy
• Crisis assets to cover family calamities
• Family Subsidizes hold in the event that something occurs with your work or you
• Is your retirement not far off?

This step fills in as an establishment for fostering your arrangement and gives you a decent reference highlight to accomplish your short as well as long-haul monetary objectives.

2) Decide Monetary Objectives

Specialists say when you have distinguished your objectives; you're probably going to accomplish them. Featuring the monetary objectives fills in as a significant part of monetary preparation. Exposed to what progressively ease in life you have reached, these objectives could be:

• Get hitched and start a family

• Buy or pay off a property

• Guarantee your youngsters get a well-rounded schooling

• Make your stores and speculations charge capable

• Get retirement with enough pay on hand to appreciate life ahead

The sole reason for this step is to separate your necessities from your needs. Aside from these, the objectives or goals might go from spending your whole pay to fostering a durable speculation program for future monetary security. In any case, you should choose which objectives you want to seek after.

3) Distinguish Choices for Venture

After an intensive comprehension of your monetary requirements has been taken and every one of the suitable monetary objectives has been established next thing is the speculation options or explicit proposals from your monetary organizer.

By looking closely at your short, medium, and long-haul objectives, a coordinated speculation methodology would be created in light of your set prerequisites. Moreover, the targets would be viewed once more and will be dissected in a way in which far you are not too far off to accomplish your short and long-haul monetary objectives. Considering your time period, income, risk resilience, current protection inclusion, charge procedures, and speculation objectives, the scope of thoughts and monetary arranging choices would be introduced to figure out which one suits you the best. This will assist you with delivering more real and fulfilling choices.

4) Assess Choices

The proposed suggestions are then additionally surveyed. This is your opportunity to talk about the options eye to eye and make vital moves remembering what is happening, monetary standings, and individual interests. Assuming you have any worries in regard to your monetary organizer's suggestions, those can be adjusted and reconsidered. Options can be shut down in light of the choices you make. For example:

The plan to carry on your schooling validates you can't do regular work. Dynamic consequently remains as a continuous cycle which works one next to the other with your own monetary circumstance so lost open doors because of your direction ought to constantly be remembered while breaking down the other options.

Risk Assessment

While assessing the choices you could wind up having dubious thoughts. For example, picking your profession over examinations implies risk. How might you guarantee to assume that it's remunerating in your future?

Other monetary choices include a nearly low level of hazard, for example, setting aside your cash in an investment account or buying some object of extraordinary worth with it. The choice of losing that article is low in such situations.

Subsequently while pursuing monetary choices; figuring out dangers is interesting to assess them. You really want to gather information in light of your experience and the encounters of others too. The dynamic cycle will expect you to as often as possible update your insight strategically, monetarily, and socially so you can settle on informed choices.

5) Set up a Monetary Arrangement and Carryout
When you are happy with the proposals and feel better to continue, the execution of the arrangement would be completed. This step of the monetary arranging cycle can be considered as an activity plan where you will pick ways of accomplishing your short, prompt, or long-haul objectives. Frequently made as the hardest stride for certain individuals, yet has a gigantic effect over the long haul!
The critical interesting point here is to do it as soon as possible. The more it's left unattended, the more it will take you to develop your riches - eventually, an extraordinary shortage in your reserve funds when you resign.

6) Audit, Reconsider, and Screen The Arrangement
Monetary arranging is an ongoing and dynamic cycle and it's improbable that your monetary condition will stay the same all through your life. You really want to evaluate your monetary choices occasionally as a changed individual, financial and

social variables will expect you to modify your choices to squeeze into your new circumstance.

As you progress through the various periods of your life, your monetary requirements will be reflected and monetary interaction will act as an instrument to allow you to conform to these changes. Checking your arrangements will assist you with focusing on your choices and cause important changes that will align your monetary necessities and objectives with your ongoing life circumstance.

Parts of a decent monetary arrangement
Monetary objectives:

You can't make an arrangement until you understand what you need to achieve with your cash — so whether you're making it yourself or working with an expert, your arrangement ought, to begin with, a rundown of your objectives, both of all shapes and sizes. It can assist with sorting out them by how long you'll require the cash:

Transient objectives are those you desire to accomplish in the following five years — like taking care of obligations or purchasing another vehicle.

Medium-term objectives are those you desire to accomplish in the following five to 10 years — like the initial installment on a home or going into business.

Long haul objectives are those that are at least 10 years away — including school and, obviously, retirement.

For every objective, determine a dollar figure and a deadline.

A large group of online instruments can assist you with running the numbers, weighing contending needs, and deciding the best strategy for you. Furthermore, in the event that you have various objectives to pursue, a robot guide, or computerized financial planning stage, can assist you with gauging the significance of every objective, positioning them by requirements, needs, and wishes.

1. Any time is a great chance to lay out a monetary arrangement.

In a perfect world, you begin putting for monetary objectives right off the bat throughout everyday life, except any time is a great opportunity to monitor what is going on and evaluate how you're doing — Would you say you are still on target? Do you have different objectives you hadn't recently thought of? Having a monetary arrangement assists you with evaluating where you are today and where you need to go straight away.

2. Total assets proclamation

Each plan needs a standard, so next, you ought to decide your total assets. Make a rundown of every one of your resources (bank and speculation accounts, land, important individual property) and another of every one of your obligations (Mastercards, contracts, understudy loans). Your resources short your liabilities rises to your total assets.

3. Financial plan and income arranging

Your financial plan is truly where everything becomes real, arranging-wise. It can assist you with figuring out where your cash is going and where you can scale once again to meet your objectives.

A spending plan number cruncher can assist with guaranteeing you don't disregard sporadic yet significant costs, for example, vehicle fixes, personal medical services expenses, and land charges. As you're accumulating your rundown, separate your costs into two cans: must-have things like food and lease, and pleasant to-haves, for example, eating out and exercise center enrollments.

While thinking about how your objectives fit into your financial plan, you might need to pressure-test it utilizing "consider the possibility that" situations: Imagine a scenario where you need or have to resign prior. Imagine a scenario where you cut back on your home loan. Some robot consultants offer apparatuses that permit you to change specific presumptions to perceive what they could mean for your reserve funds technique.

4. Obligation the executives plan

obligation once in a while dealing with like a four-letter word, yet not all obligation is terrible obligation. A home loan, for instance, can assist with developing value — and help your FICO rating in the deal. Exorbitant interest customer obligation like Mastercards, then again, weighs vigorously on your FICO assessment. Besides, every dollar you pay in finance charges and premium is one you can't put toward different objectives.

In the event that you have an exorbitant interest obligation, ensure you make an arrangement that can assist you with taking care of it as fast as could be expected. In the event that you don't know where to begin, a monetary counselor can assist you with focusing on, then deciding the amount of your spending plan ought to go toward your obligations every month.

5. Retirement plan

An old guideline says you'll require roughly 80% of your current pay in retirement. Nonetheless, this accepts that resigning will liberate you from any business-related costs and charges, that you've taken care of your home loan, and that your kids will be monetarily free.

It's likewise essential to remember that Government medical care doesn't cover everything, and medical services expenses that Federal medical insurance doesn't cover — like long haul care — can add up rapidly. You likewise could spend more on different things in retirement, similar as travel, feasting out, gifts, or monetary help to a family member or companion.

Connecting various situations into a retirement reserve funds mini-computer can assist you with sorting out what you might require in retirement.

Try not to rely on the 80% rule

In the event that you're saving 20-30% of your pre-retirement pay, the 80% pay substitution rule is a decent spot to begin. In any case, it's more secure to target covering 100 percent of your pre-retirement pay, less anything that you're putting something aside for retirement. Similarly, as with any overall guideline, there are a lot of special cases. So make certain to plunk down and tweak your retirement spending plan as the time moves close. This ought to be your first concern since you can get it for most different objectives but not so much for retirement.

6. Crisis reserves

When something startling occurs — you lose your employment, for instance, or get hit with a surprising doctor's visit expense — a secret stash can assist you with trying not to tap your drawn-out investment funds to earn barely enough to get by.

It's by and large smart to save to the point of covering no less than 90 days — except for preferably a half year's — worth of fundamental everyday costs (e.g., food, lodging, transportation, and utilities). Set aside this cash in a profoundly fluid checking or bank account so you can get to it in a rush should the need emerge.

7. Protection inclusion

Protection is a significant piece of safeguarding your monetary disadvantage — yet neither would it be a good idea for you to overpay for inclusion you needn't bother with. Overall:

Medical coverage: Without it, even routine consideration can cost a chunk of change, while a serious physical issue or emergency clinic stay could hinder you a huge number of dollars. As you progress in years, you might need to think about long-haul care protection, too.

Handicap protection: This inclusion safeguards you and your family on the occasion you can't work. Boss gave inability protection regularly replaces around 60% of your compensation.

Auto and mortgage holders'/leaseholders' protection: In the event that you own a vehicle or home — or lease and can't bear to supplant assets using cash on hand — ensure you're enough safeguarded.

Disaster protection: This is for the most part smart for those with wards. Work with a protection specialist to comprehend what kind of — and how much — inclusion checks out for you.

8. Domain plan

At least, you ought to have a will, which expresses your last wishes concerning your resources, wards, and who you need to direct your domain. YouJYou ought to likewise keep the recipients of your insurance contracts and retirement accounts exceptional. Likewise consider laying out legal authorities for monetary and medical care choices, for the situation you become debilitated.

The Most Effective Method To Make A Monetary Strategies And Adheres To Its

We've all been there. A few of us didn't save more when we were more youthful, others began saving and spent everything in under five years. In the event that we knew, what we know currently about having an arrangement for each Dollars procured, things would have been totally different for ourselves and numerous others.

Regardless, making a legitimate monetary blueprint is dependably an objective.

To accomplish this objective, you should:

Be Express: Don't gloss over the circumstance. Be straightforward with yourself about your ongoing monetary standing.

Put forth Basic Objectives: Clear and straightforward objectives are simpler to recollect and execute. Love yourself enough to keuep it basic.

Try not to rehash your errors of the past. Fabricate a monetary strategy today

Make a monetary blueprint: Working with a specialist
Winning plays are not only for sports groups. Regular financial backers need procedures for progress, as well. Consider these five inquiries as you start constructing or exploring your monetary course of action.

1. Do I really want a monetary specialist?
Normally, yes. Monetary advisors accomplish something beyond assisting with your speculations. They assist you with anticipating your monetary future. A monetary specialist can assist with abundance conservation matters like domain arranging and trust designation.

2. How would I pick a monetary specialist?
A decent spot to begin is to ask loved ones for suggestions. On the other hand, you can set up a gathering with the Head's expert to examine your monetary requirements and objectives.

3. What would it be a good idea for me to bring to my gathering?

Whether this is your most memorable gathering with a specialist or a registration with your current expert, boost your time by getting ready ahead. Get some information about unambiguous reports you ought to bring, if necessary.

4. What inquiries would it be advisable for me to pose?

Perhaps you need to reprioritize your financial plan, save more, or survey your retirement arranging technique. Ponder any monetary inquiries, regardless of how huge or little, and record them somewhat early.

In the event that this is your most memorable time working with an expert, make sure to ask them inquiries. Furthermore, don't be timid about asking what their charges are, the same token. It is critical to know how they hope to be paid for their administrations.

5. How frequently would it be a good idea for me to meet with my specialist?

Whenever you have a monetary blueprint set up, take a break once per year to survey and refresh your arrangement. Significant life-altering situations and changing objectives might mean you want to change your monetary plays.

Making a Monetary Strategy | An Achievement-Based Manual for an Exceptional Necessities Plan

Extraordinary Necessities Plan

The expansion of a youngster with extraordinary requirements to your family can bring a scope of feelings. With time the feelings can settle, however, the obligation of accommodating your developing family frequently grabs hold. Making a monetary arrangement with a believed consultant is basic, and showing up at different achievements can direct you in what to do straight away. The following are seven achievements to benchmark your arranging endeavors with monetary guidance for each defining moment.

1 - At determination:

Blueprint Stages BabyThe first thing to recollect at determination is to quiet your considerations and try not to settle on any abrupt monetary choices or massive changes. The progressions to your family will probably bring about the requirement for monetary change, yet they don't need to happen at the same time.

Begin by attempting to instruct yourself on your kid's determination, fabricating a base of information to later arrange for his/her drawn-out needs. An extraordinary method for doing this is to find an emotionally supportive network, whether that be a parent support bunch, determination explicit associations, or other local gatherings.

On the off chance that there is one monetary change that can be made immediately, starting to construct cash saves is a praiseworthy objective, particularly on the off chance that you don't as of now have a sound secret stash. For most families, this isn't something that should be possible at the same time, however, perceive that spontaneous costs might come up for the consideration and backing of your kid. Having cash accessible to deal with these spontaneous costs might save you from being required to settle on troublesome monetary choices later because of assuming obligation or constrained account redistributions.

2 - Think about the Long haul:

Choosing to address what befalls your kid in the event that something happens to you is difficult for some guardians, so tracking down the energy to draft a will and trust can challenge. That is the reason this direction isn't attached to a benchmark and is rather something we would urge a family to address when they are sincerely prepared.

Whenever you are ready to examine this, draw in a certified lawyer who zeros in their training on extraordinary requirements arranging. Work through the drafting of a will to name gatekeepers for your minor youngsters, and talk through a family trust to deal with the conveyance of your resources. Furthermore, assuming you expect that your kid might fit the bill for SSI or different backings, consider a unique necessities trust to assist with saving qualification. When the trust work is altogether your occupation is unfinished until you have changed each of the recipient assignments to mirror this work.

3 - As your youngster arrives at a young:

This time can give a snapshot of monetary delay for guardians, where the emphasis may be on early mediation for your youngster and the planning to begin school. However, that monetary respite rapidly disperses assuming you are sufficiently lucky to have choices while thinking about your kid's necessities. The cost related to tuition-based school choices brings up various monetary issues. Might you at any point manage the cost of these choices, do the catered administrations to your kid's finding legitimize the cost, and what are the drawn-out monetary effects of these choices? The whole family should be thought about while thoroughly considering the effect on retirement, future instruction financing, and the capacity to pass on resources for an exceptional necessities trust.

As you work through your Individualized Instruction Program with the region, consider what openings may be passed on to fill through confidential administrations. The IEP will foster the center's daily schedule and backing structure for your kid, yet what else could you have to coordinate beyond the school day and how do those administrations fit in the family financial plan?

4 - Your Kid Turns 18:

A major progress for guardians and youngsters is the same happens when your kid turns 18 and turns into a grown-up. Perhaps the most squeezing task is acquiring a comprehension of what government-backed retirement is and what it can give, both now and later on.

This money advantage can assist with supporting the family and accommodate your kid's necessities, yet in addition, accompanies prerequisites. You want to know how to report the receipt and utilization of the assets, consider charging your kid lease to save the full month-to-month benefit sum, and furthermore deal with the collection of the cash so it doesn't surpass resource limitations.

5 - After Secondary School:

Approach Stages GraduateIt's during this time you need to attempt to try not to fall into the "dark opening" that can shape when you leave the everyday design of the educational system. Are there present auxiliary instruction choices to consider, and assuming this is the case how would you execute the subsidizing technique that ought to have been made a very long time earlier? In the event that some type of school or professional advancement isn't fitting, are there business choices accessible to your kid? These choices can come as a full or part-time business, or conceivably through work programs intended to increment freedom, all with a differing influence on your youngster's (and in this manner you are) funds.

It's as of now that you ought to start to acquire some lucidity concerning what your kid's monetary necessities will be going ahead, so as a family you can start to truly make arrangements for how you will enhance what your kid has accessible through government-backed retirement and potentially business. Interestingly you can start to perceive how much your kid will require in their trust.

The monetary arranging turns out to be always significant during these years, on the grounds that while many are partaking in their pinnacle acquiring years and saving more for retirement than previously, the freshly discovered lucidity of what could be left in trust for your kid can scare. Putting something aside for our own retirement can be challenging enough for some, so adding the subsidizing for a unique necessities trust to the situation requires an elevated degree of concentration and particular direction.

6 - Entering Adulthood:

Blueprint Stages HouseAs you approach a period of pinnacle freedom for your kid, private choices can now turn into a thought. Finding the suitable choice with your youngster takes devotion and time, and subsidizing these choices can take something very similar. Is the best answer for your family supported through government-backed retirement, does it require private installment or is it a blend of the two?

7 - Sometime down the road:

Now is the ideal time to be sure that your home is altogether. In the wake of illustrating each of the potential expenses prior, comprehend that these costs don't end when you are presently not here to accommodate them. Your cash doesn't simply need to keep going as long as you do, however long your kid needs it. Verify you have searched out the guidance of a counselor experienced in assisting you with accomplishing this. Monetary projections could run for a really long time slonger than your life expectancy to get your youngster's future appropriately.

Likewise, invest important energy ensuring you have empowered future guardians and legal administrators to do what you have requested from them. Have you represented each of your resources in a concentrated area, complete with the monetary projections that were the groundwork of your choices? Are essential records coordinated? An opportunity to coordinate individuals that will be your youngster's future emotionally supportive network is currently.

Despite which achievement you are at, realize that you are in good company. Make sure to assets and connect with a confided-in consultant to assist you with exploring the open doors and difficulties together. Cautious arranging is critical, and understanding achievements can assist with guaranteeing a smoother change from one achievement to another and an inward feeling of harmony.

Chapter Three

Effective Financial Planning

What is Speculation?

A venture is a resource or thing gathered fully intent on producing pay or acknowledgment. From a financial viewpoint, speculation is the acquisition of products that are not consumed today yet are utilized in the future to create riches. In finance, a venture is a monetary resource purchased with the possibility that the resource will turn out revenue further or will later be sold at a greater expense cost for a benefit.

Speculation is clarified and characterized as an expansion to the store of actual capital, for example,

- Hardware
- Structures
- Streets and so forth.,

for example, anything that summarizes the future useful capacity of the economy and changes in the list (or a load of completed items) of a maker. Note that 'speculation wares' (like machines) are additionally important for the last items - they are not halfway products like unrefined components. Machines fabricated in an economy in a given year are not 'utilized something like' produce different wares but yield their administrations over various years.

Speculation choices by producers, for example, whether to purchase new hardware, depend generally, on the available spot pace of interest. Nonetheless, for effortlessness, we assume here that ventures intend to contribute a similar sum consistently. We can compose the ex-bet speculation interest as:

10 Normal Kinds of Speculations and How They Work

Contributing can scare many individuals since there are numerous choices and it tends to be difficult to sort out which ventures are ideal for your portfolio. This guide strolls you through ten of the most well-known sorts of ventures, from stocks to wares, and makes sense of why you might need to consider remembering each for your portfolio. In the event that you're signed in money management, it could check out to find a monetary consultant who can direct you and assist you with sorting out which ventures will assist you with coming to your goals.

1. Stocks

Stocks, otherwise called offers or values, maybe the most notable and basic kind of venture. At the point when you purchase stock, you're purchasing a possession stake in a public corporation. A significant number of the greatest organizations in the nation are public, meaning you can purchase stock in them.

How you can bring in cash: When you purchase a stock, you're trusting that the cost will go up so you can then sell it for a benefit. The gamble, obviously, is that the cost of the stock could go down, in which case you'd lose cash.

2. Bonds

At the point when you purchase a security, you're basically loaning cash to a substance. By and large, this is a business or an administration element. Organizations issue corporate securities, while nearby legislatures issue civil securities. The U.S.

Depository issues Depository bonds, notes, and bills, which are all obligation instruments that financial backers purchase.

How you can bring in cash: While the cash is being loaned, the bank or financial backer gets revenue instalments. After the bond develops, the significance you've held it for the legally resolved measure of time, you get your chief back.

The pace of return for bonds is ordinarily much lower than it is for stocks, however, bonds likewise will generally be a lower risk. There is still some gambling required, obviously. The organization you purchase a bond from could crease or the public authority could default. Depository bonds, notes, and bills, nonetheless, are viewed as extremely safe ventures

3. Shared Assets

A shared asset is a pool of many financial backers' cash that is put extensively into various organizations. Common assets can be effectively overseen or inactively made due. An effectively overseen reserve has an asset chief who picks protections in which to put financial backers' cash. Store supervisors frequently attempt to beat an assigned market list by picking ventures that will outflank such a file. A latently oversaw reserve, otherwise called a file store, basically tracks a significant financial exchange record. Common assets can put resources into an expansive exhibit of protections: values, bonds, products, monetary standards, and subordinates.

Common subsidies convey a considerable lot of similar dangers as stocks and bonds, contingent upon what they are put resources into. The gamble is frequently lesser, however, on the grounds that the speculations are intrinsically differentiated.

How you can bring in cash: Financial backers bring in cash off common assets when the worth of stocks, securities, and other packaged protections that the asset puts resources into go up. You can get them straightforwardly through the overseeing firm and markdown financiers. However, note there is normally a base speculation and you'll pay a yearly charge.

4. Trade Exchanged Assets

Trade exchanged reserves are like shared assets in that they are an assortment of speculations that tracks a market file. Not at all like common assets, which are bought through an asset organization, portions of Trade Exchanged Assets are traded on financial exchanges. Their cost changes all through the exchanging day, while common subsidizes' worth is just the net resource worth of your ventures, which is determined toward the finish of each exchanging meeting.

How you can bring in cash: Trade Exchanged Assets bring in cash from the assortment of a return among their interests in general. Trade Exchanged Assets are frequently prescribed to new financial backers since they're more broadened than individual stocks. You can additionally limit risk by picking an Trade Exchanged Asset that tracks an expansive record. What's more, very much like shared reserves, you can bring in cash from an Trade Exchanged Assets by selling it as it acquires esteem.

5. Declarations of Store

A testament of the store is viewed as an extremely generally safe venture. You give a bank a specific measure of cash for a foreordained measure of time and bring in revenue on that cash. At the point when that time span is finished, you get your chief back, in addition to the foreordained measure of interest.

The more drawn out the advance time frame, the higher your loan fee is probably going to be. While the gamble is low, the potential return is as well.

How you can bring in cash: With a Compact disc, you bring in cash from the premium that you procure during the term of the store. Albums are great long-haul ventures for setting aside cash.

6. Retirement Plans

A retirement plan is a venture account, with specific tax reductions, where financial backers put away their cash for retirement. There are various sorts of retirement plans, for example, working environment retirement plans, supported by your boss. On the off chance that you don't approach a business-supported retirement plan, you could get a singular retirement plan.

How you can bring in cash: Retirement plans are definitely not a different class of venture, fundamentally, yet a vehicle to purchase stocks, securities, and assets in two duty-advantaged ways. The first, allows you to contribute pretax dollars (similar to a conventional IRA). The second permits you to pull out cash without paying charges on that cash. The dangers for the ventures are equivalent to on the off chance that you were purchasing the speculations beyond a retirement plan.

7. Choices

A choice is a to some degree further developed or complex method for purchasing a stock. At the point when you purchase a choice, you're buying the capacity to trade a resource at a specific cost at a given time. There are two kinds of choices: call choices, for purchasing resources, and put choices, for selling choices.

How you can bring in cash: As a financial backer, you secure the cost of a stock with the expectation that it will go up in esteem. Notwithstanding, the gamble of a choice is that the stock could likewise lose cash. So assuming the stock abatements from its underlying cost, you lose the cash of the agreement. Choices are a high-level money management strategy and retail ought to practice alert prior to utilizing them.

8. Annuities

At the point when you purchase an annuity, you buy an insurance contract and, consequently, you get occasional installments. These installments by and large descend the street in retirement however much of the time bought a very long time ahead of time. To this end, many individuals use annuities as a component of their retirement reserve funds plans.

Annuities come in various assortments. They might go on til' the very end or just for a foreordained timeframe. They might require occasional premium installments or only one front-and-center installment. They might connect somewhat to the financial exchange or they may basically be an insurance contract with no immediate connection to the business sectors. Installments might be quick or conceded to a predefined date. They might be fixed or variable.

How you can bring in cash: Annuities can ensure an extra stream of pay for retirement. In any case, while they are genuinely okay, they aren't high-development. So financial backers will generally make them a decent enhancement for their retirement investment funds, instead of an indispensable wellspring of subsidizing.

9. Subsidiary

A subsidiary is a monetary instrument that drives its worth from another resource. Like an annuity, it is an agreement between two gatherings. For this situation, however, the agreement is consent to sell a resource at a particular cost from here on out. On the off chance that the financial backer consents to buy the subordinate, they are wagering that the worth won't diminish. Subordinates are viewed as a further developed venture and are regularly bought by institutional financial backers.

The three most normal kinds of subsidiaries are:

Choices Agreements: The choices contract offers the financial backer the chance to trade a resource at a particular cost at a particular time from now on. Call choices give you the chance to purchase the resource costing that much and put choices permit you to sell that resource.

Prospects Agreements: Fates are getting that focus on a deal being made at a predefined time and on a predetermined date.

Trades: This is an arrangement between two gatherings to trade incomes later on.

How you can bring in cash: You can bring in cash putting resources into subordinates on the off chance that you are on the right half of cost changes. For instance, assuming you consent to purchase copper at $1,000 in nine months however the market cost around then is $2,000 then you've basically multiplied your venture.

10. Items

Items are actual items that you can put resources into. They are normal in fates markets where makers and business purchasers - all in all, experts - try to support their monetary stake in the items.

Retail financial backers ought to ensure they completely figure out prospects prior to putting resources into them. Halfway, that is on the grounds that items contributing runs the gamble that the cost of ware will move pointedly and unexpectedly in one or the other bearing because of abrupt occasions. For example, political activities can enormously change the benefit of something like oil, while the weather conditions can influence the worth of farming items.

Here is a breakdown of the four principal kinds of items:

- **Metals:** valuable metals (gold and silver) and modern metals (copper)
- **Agrarian:** Wheat, corn, and soybeans
- **Animals:** Pork tummies and feeder dairy cattle
- **Energy:** Raw petroleum, oil-based commodities, and flammable gas

How you can bring in cash: The essential way that financial backers bring in cash with wares is by exchanging item prospects. Financial backers once in a while purchase wares as a support for their portfolios during expansion. You can purchase items in a roundabout way through stocks and common assets and fates contracts.

The most effective method to Purchase Various Kinds of Speculations

There are two fundamental ways for you to buy the various sorts of ventures you might be keen on purchasing, however, one way or the other will expect you to have a functioning speculation account. Each is not difficult to do, yet only one of the two offers support that is totally finished for you.

The two general ways of purchasing the sorts of speculations you need are:

- Begin an Internet-based Money market fund: You can choose to deal with your own speculations and simply open a money market fund. This empowers you to make ready rapidly with the capacity to purchase stock, securities, shared assets, and more in no time flat. The main disadvantage is that you'll pursue the last monetary choices generally all alone.

- Employ a Monetary Consultant: The alternate method for purchasing different sorts of ventures is to recruit a monetary counselor. The guide can not just give you admittance to purchase and exchange resources however they can likewise assist you with sorting out an in-general monetary procedure and set you up enough for retirement. This is a greater amount of a computerized cycle in that you simply need to support exchanges or ventures and the counselor deals with the subtleties. Your guide can assist you with getting a money market fund, depending on the situation.

Most well-known sorts of ventures and how they work

There are various sorts of the venture to browse. Some are ideal for novices, while others require more insight and examination. Each kind of speculation offers an alternate degree of chance and prize, giving you a decent choice or two regardless of what your objective may be. Financial backers ought to consider each kind of venture prior to deciding on a resource portion that lines up with their by and large monetary objectives.

Contributing Tips

It can some of the time help to have a specialist in your corner while effective money management. Finding a certified monetary guide doesn't need to be hard. SmartAsset's free device coordinates you with up to three verified monetary guides who serve your region, and you can meet with your counsellor matches at no expense to conclude which one is ideal for you. In the event that you're prepared to find a counsellor who can assist you with accomplishing your monetary objectives, get everything rolling at this point.

In the event that your speculations pay off, you might owe the capital additions charge. Sort out the amount you'll pay when you sell your stocks with our capital increases charge-adding machine.

Instructions to Put away Cash: Picking the Most ideal Way To Contribute for You

Putting cash in the financial exchange is the No. 1 way Americans create financial well-being and save for long-haul objectives like retirement, however sorting out the best methodology to put away that cash can feel overwhelming.

The most ideal way to put away cash: A bit-by-bit guide

Everybody has what is going on. The most ideal way to contribute relies upon your own inclinations alongside your current and future monetary conditions. Having an itemized comprehension of your pay and costs, resources and liabilities, obligations, and objectives while building a sound money management plan is significant.

Here is a five-step process that can assist you with sorting out some way to put away your cash at the present time:

- Recognize your monetary objectives, time period, and sentiments about risk.

- Conclude whether you need to take a "DIY" or "oversee it for me" approach.
- Pick the sort of venture account you'll utilize
- Open a record.
- Pick a mix of ventures that match your gamble resilience and give expansion (stocks, securities, common assets, land).

What's more, here are the subtleties on the best way to give your money something to do in the correct manner, immediately.

Prepared to begin money management? Find out about the best ventures at the present time

1. Give your cash an objective
Sorting out some way to put away cash begins with deciding your effective money management objectives when you want or need to accomplish them, and your solace level with risk for every objective.

Long-haul objectives: These objectives are no less than five years away. The all-inclusive objective is many times retirement, however, you might have others too: Do you need an initial installment on a house or schooling cost? To buy your fantasy country estate or go on a commemoration trip in 10 years?

Transient objectives: These objectives are under five years away. This is the following year's get-away, a house you need to purchase one year from now, a backup stash, or your Christmas stash. Cash for transient objectives by and large ought not to be contributed by any means. Assuming you really want the cash you're saving in less than five years, look at our proposals for how to put away cash for transient objectives.

Here, we're generally zeroing in on long-haul objectives. We'll likewise address how to put in view no particular objective. All things considered, the expectation to develop your cash is a fine objective without anyone else.

» Inquisitive about purchasing stocks? Work out how to put finances into the securities dealing.

2. Conclude how much assistance you with needing

When you know your objectives, you can plunge into the particulars about how to contribute (from picking the kind of record to the best spot to open a record to picking venture vehicles). Be that as it may, on the off chance that the Do-It-Yourself course doesn't seem as though it'll be your favorite, no problem.

Numerous savers lean toward having somebody put away their cash for them. And keeping in mind that that used to be an expensive suggestion, these days it's very reasonable — modest, even! — to enlist proficient assistance because of the appearance of the computerized portfolio of the executive's administrations.

These web-based counselors use PC calculations and high-level programming to construct and deal with a client's venture portfolio, offering everything from programmed rebalancing to burden streamlining and even admittance to human assistance when you really want it.

Best speculations for fledglings
1. High-return investment accounts

This can be one of the easiest ways of helping the profit from your cash above the thing you're procuring in a normal financial record. High-return bank accounts, which are in many cases opened through a web-based bank, will generally pay a higher premium on normal than standard bank accounts while as yet giving clients ordinary admittance to their cash.

This can be an extraordinary spot to stop cash you're putting something aside for a buy in the two or three years or simply holding in the event of a crisis.

2. Declarations of the store

Discs are one more method for procuring extra revenue on your investment funds, however, they will tie up your cash for longer than a high-return bank account. You can buy a Cd for various time spans like a half year, one year, or even five years, yet you commonly can't get to the cash before the Compact disc develops without suffering a consequence.

These are viewed as very protected and on the off chance that you buy one through a governmentally safeguarded bank, you're concealed to $250,000 per contributor, per proprietorship class.

3. Another work environment retirement plan

This can be one of the easiest ways of getting everything rolling in financial planning and accompanies a few significant motivations that could help you now and later on. Most businesses deal to match a piece of what you consent to put something aside for retirement out of your normal check. On the off chance that your manager offers a match and you don't take part in the arrangement, you are turning down free cash.

These work environment retirement plans are extraordinary reserve funds apparatuses on the grounds that they're programmed whenever you've made your underlying determinations and permit you to contribute over the long run reliably. Frequently, you might in fact decide to put resources into deadline common assets, which deal with their portfolios in view of a particular retirement date. As you draw nearer to the deadline, the asset's portion will move away from more hazardous resources to represent a more limited speculation skyline.

away from more dangerous resources for representing a more limited speculation skyline.

4. Common assets

Common subsidies offer financial backers the chance to put resources into a bushel of stocks or bonds (or different resources) that they probably won't have the option to effectively expand all alone.

The most well-known shared reserves track records, for example, the S&P 500, which is contained around 500 of the biggest organizations in the U.S. File finances as a rule accompany exceptionally low charges for the assets' financial backers, and sporadically no expense by any stretch of the imagination. These low costs assist financial backers with saving a greater amount of the assets' profits for them and can be an extraordinary method for creating financial stability over the long run.

5. Trade Exchanged Assets

Trade exchanged assets, are like shared assets in that they hold a bushel of protection, however, they exchange over the course of the day the same way a stock would. Trade Exchanged Assets don't accompany similar least speculation necessities as shared reserves, which regularly come in at two or three thousand bucks. Trade Exchanged Assets can be bought for the expense of one offer in addition to any charges or commissions related to the buy, however, you can get everything rolling with even less assuming your specialist permits fragmentary offer financial planning.

6. Individual stocks

Purchasing stocks in individual organizations is the least secure speculation choice examined here, yet it can likewise be one of the most fulfilling. Be that as it may, before you begin making exchanges, you ought to consider whether purchasing a stock seems OK for you. Inquire as to whether you are financial planning as long as possible, which by and large means somewhere around five years, and whether you comprehend the business you are putting resources into. Stocks are evaluated the entire exchanging day and hence, individuals frequently get brought into the momentary exchanging attitude when they own singular stocks.

In any case, a stock is a fractional proprietorship stake in a genuine business and over the long run your fortune will ascend with that of the hidden organization you put resources into. On the off chance that you don't feel you have the mastery or stomach to brave it with individual stocks, consider adopting the more expanded strategy presented by shared assets or Trade Exchanged Assets all things considered.

For what reason would it be advisable for you to begin money management?

Contributing is critical if you have any desire to keep up with the buying influence of your investment funds and arrive at long-haul monetary objectives like retirement or creating financial stability. On the off chance that you let your reserve funds sit in a conventional financial balance procuring practically no premium, at last expansion will diminish the worth of your well-deserved cash. By putting resources into resources like stocks and securities, you can ensure your investment funds stay aware of expansion or even outperforms it.

Transient speculations like high-return bank accounts or currency market shared assets can assist you with procuring more on your investment funds while you pursue a major buy like a vehicle or an upfront installment on a house. Stocks and Trade Exchanged Assets are viewed as better for long-haul objectives like retirement since they are bound to procure better returns over the long haul, yet they convey extra gamble.

Significant contemplations for new financial backers

- **Risk resilience:** Before you begin financial planning, you'll need to grasp your own capacity to bear risk. Unstable speculations, for example, stocks can make certain individuals truly awkward when they decline, which can make you sell at the absolute worst time. Knowing your gamble resilience will assist you with picking which speculations are the most ideal for you.

- **Monetary objectives:** Lay out both short-and long haul objectives that you need to accomplish through saving and money management. Understanding your objectives will assist you with fostering a strong arrangement.

- **Dynamic or inactive:** You'll likewise have to choose if you might want to be a latent financial backer or a functioning one. A detached financial backer regularly possesses a resource like broadened common assets that charge low expenses, while a functioning financial backer could pick individual speculations or shared reserves that intend to outflank the market. Studies have shown that detached money management will in general beat dynamic financial planning over the long run.

- **Enlist somebody:** You can likewise decide to deal with your own speculations through a web-based intermediary, or recruit a monetary counselor to take care of you. You'll probably cause lower costs on the off chance that you do it without anyone's help, however, a consultant can be useful for those simply beginning.

- **Charges:** Assuming you own interests in an individual or shared service, you'll probably have to pay charges on the premium, profits, and capital additions you procure. You can keep away from these duties by possessing interests in charge of advantaged retirement records.

How much cash is expected to begin effective financial planning?

Fortunately, you don't require a lot of cash to begin effective money management. Most internet-based representatives have no record essentials to begin and some propositions partially offer financial planning for those beginning with little dollar sums.

For only a couple of dollars, you can buy Trade exchanged assets that permit you to construct an expanded arrangement of stocks. Miniature financial planning stages will try and let you gather together buys made through a check card as a method for getting everything rolling with effective money management.

In the event that you're simply beginning in the speculation world, make a point to consider your gamble resistance and what your monetary objectives are prior to committing cash to a venture. A few ventures, similar to high-return bank accounts, consider speedy admittance to cash on the off chance that crises come up. In the meantime, stocks ought to presumably be essential for a drawn-out money growth strategy all things considered.

How Might I Begin Money management?

You can pick the do-it yourself course, choose speculations in light of your financial planning style, or enroll with the assistance of a venture proficient, like a counselor or dealer. Prior to effective financial planning, it's vital to figure out what your inclinations and chance resistance are. In the event that risk-unwilling, picking stocks and choices, may not be the most ideal decision. Foster a technique, framing the amount to contribute, how frequently to contribute, and what to put resources into in view of objectives and inclinations. Prior to allotting your assets, research the objective speculation to ensure it lines up with your technique and can possibly convey wanted results. Keep in mind, you needn't bother with a truckload of cash to start, and you can alter as your requirements change.

Chapter Four:

Procuring

Profit is how much cash you make from finishing work. You'll be significantly more amped up for minding you gain proficiency with your profit will be more than liberal.

Most profits come from work that you've done, in spite of the fact that cash you acquire from speculation can likewise be called profit. Any monetary benefit or gain you make goes into the income classification, since you bring in that cash, whether through work, karma, or knowledge. The Proto-Germanic root, *anon, signifies "accomplish reap work."

What is profit financial planning?

Pay money management includes building a portfolio utilizing profit-paying stocks, securities, land, and different resources intended to produce cash on a common premise. With pay financial planning, when you purchase the resource, there is definitely not significantly more to do. This is purchase-and-hold latent money management at its ideal.

There are a lot of various ways you can get cash. Some you need to work for, others your cash accomplishes the work for you. We should investigate a couple here.

- **Compensation**

This pays you to procure from a task, where you are paid an hourly rate to follow through with set responsibilities. The more hours you work, the more cash you acquire.

- **Pay**

Like wages, this is cash you procure from a task. Your yearly compensation is normally set out in an agreement and paid either week after week, fortnightly, or month to month. Typically the sum is normal and you will not procure something else for additional hours worked.

- **Commission**

The commission is where you bring in cash for getting done with a job. This is normal in deals jobs. You could bring in a limited measure of cash for every deal you make or you could procure a level of a deal cost for your work. The commission depends on results instead of time worked.

- **Interest**

Premium is something that your cash procures for you (whoopee!) Premium is normally paid on cash that you have stored with your bank. The premium differs between account types and is normally communicated as a rate each year (or per annum).

- **Selling something you make or own**

Perhaps you're convenient with a needle and string or you're a talented mathematician. You could have a lot of stuff you don't need any longer. Selling things you make, your abilities as a help, or stuff you own and never again need are ways of getting some money.

- **Speculations**

Speculations like property offer, and: craftsmanship can all bring in cash for you either through an expansion in their worth (this is called capital development) or on account of offers, by paying you a measure of cash for every offer you hold (this is known as a profit).

- **Gifts**

Who doesn't cherish money presents? Birthday events and Christmas can be incredible and in some cases surprising kinds of revenue.

- **Stipend/Pocket Cash**

Cash your adults give you consistently. They might possibly anticipate that you should take care of responsibilities as a trade-off for the moola

- **Government Installments**

Contingent upon your circumstance you might be qualified for help installments from the government Keep in mind, getting the cash is just essential for the image. How you manage your cash can be a distinct advantage.

Chapter Five:

Monetary Women's Activist Way Of Life

As the 'monetary woman's rights' development picks up speed, obviously genuine headway can't be made for however long ladies are money management not as much as men, saving less for retirement and stopping more in real money. At the point when intensified by the orientation pay hole, this outcomes in a huge deficiency, however, there's something else to monetary woman's rights besides essentially tending to these holes: ladies likewise care about where their cash is contributed and the effect it can have.

In this pragmatic and open aid, supportable speculation master Jessica Robinson demonstrates the way that, through monetary woman's rights, ladies can utilize their monetary ability to put resources into a manageable future and construct the sort of world they need to live in. With language-free clarifications and certifiable models, she demystifies the monetary administration industry, breaks down exactly what manageable financial planning is, and shows the cultural and natural effect of the speculation.

For what reason would it be a good idea for you to think often about monetary women's liberation?

Very oversaw funds are in many cases the way to progress in any grown-up's life. Exploring the monetary circle, such as covering bills, putting something aside for retirement, settling charges, and dealing with your everyday costs, is already now troublesome for all intents and purposes. Managing orientation explicit monetary battles on top of that can make it much more seriously confounding, disappointing, and insufferable.

Monetary woman's rights are tied in with tending to only that - and the sky is the limit from there - by enabling ladies to settle on their own monetary choices. Ladies are for the most part paid not as much as men, we definitely know that. In any case, they likewise may miss the mark on monetary education abilities and certainty to put away and set aside cash, step up in their professions, and deal with their funds.

Monetary proficiency begins early in life, and a few examinations have demonstrated that the disparity begins youthful: young men get more remittance than young ladies growing up - frequently for less work. That difference goes on into adulthood.

The bottom line? Ladies procure proportionately not exactly their male partners, and lower work market interest and other fundamental predispositions build that impact. Thus, ladies are undeniably more averse to contributing and creating financial well-being throughout their lives.

Remarkable Monetary Difficulties Ladies Face

Ladies face remarkable difficulties with regard to building a fruitful monetary future.

- **Disgrace**

How frequently have you been informed that discussing finances is discourteous? Or then again get some information about how much your associates are making? From early on, ladies are educated to stay silent about funds. They're instructed that in any event, getting some information about funds is impolite, as a matter of fact. It's a profoundly imbued idea established in sexism.

It's nothing unexpected that ladies embrace sensations of disgrace around cash and funds that follow them into adulthood. Be that as it may, assuming that ladies never discuss funds, how might they excel? How might they learn and develop? Ideas like compensation straightforwardness and open conversations about subjects like the pay hole, education hole, and retirement hole have as of late fired getting a move on. Meanwhile, the most ideal way to beat this disgrace is to move your viewpoint.

"At the point when you are sure about your qualities and you know your own value, and what you bring to the world, discussing money is simple. Since cash is only a statement of your qualities," Cash - or the manner in which you use it - can unquestionably be a declaration of your qualities. For instance, do you place your well-deserved check into a retirement account since you esteem well-being and security? Do you purchase garments to encourage yourself inwardly? Consider carving out the opportunity to think about the manners by which you utilize your cash and whether it lines up with your optimal qualities.

- **Absence of understanding**

How often have you begun a discussion with somebody about the securities exchange (or, rather, get hauled into a discussion by somebody who thinks they have a lot of experience with stocks) just to feel as if you don't have the foggiest idea about what the other individual is talking about? The financial exchange accompanies its own arrangement of language and jargon, and the vast majority aren't shown what words like "short" and "shared reserve" mean. Also, abundance chiefs with terrible expectations will frequently take cover behind the language to cause themselves to feel more significant by causing you to want to contribute is something you won't ever comprehend.

The initial step to turning out to be more OK with the universe of effective financial planning and funds? That's what figuring out in spite of the fact that it might appear to be unnerving or scary, as a general rule, it's significantly surprisingly direct.

In all actuality ladies have every one of the conduct attributes to become extraordinary financial backers to set up their monetary future. It's alright not to have a deep understanding of the securities exchange - at times, you simply have to begin and sort it out leisurely, or enroll the assistance of a guide you trust.

- **Absence of direction**

Ladies don't get similar monetary exhortation and monetary direction as men, making it harder for ladies to make monetary progress sometime down the road. Most ladies growing up don't get sufficient training or support about funds. That implies they might be offered more costly monetary items when they truly do see a monetary consultant. It can likewise mean getting less schooling about monetary financial planning and planning

"Monetary schooling can dismay. There are 1,000,000 methods for procuring 1,000,000 bucks, however, where does one begin as a lady in business? Could monetary consultants at any point be relied upon, or would they say they are quantity and commission-driven? We can assume command over our monetary future and the best spot to begin is by teaching ourselves.

For what reason is monetary autonomy significant for ladies?

At the point when you deal with your own pay and plan for your own monetary future, you have undeniably more ability to settle on your own decisions throughout everyday life. Might it be said that you are needing to have a child? Would you like to venture to the far corners of the planet for a long time? Would you like to zero in on your vocation? Do you need These things? These life decisions can redirect your life, and funds empower you to go with those choices for yourself. You don't need to be subject to another person's cash on the off chance that you would rather not - regardless of whether you're hitched.

It's particularly significant in light of the fact that the monetary imbalance among people goes on all throughout their entire lives. Furthermore, throughout the span of their lives, ladies frequently end up with fewer retirement investment funds than men regardless of living far longer.

How Might You Assume Command Over Your Monetary Future?

Monetary woman's rights help tackle the fundamental foundations by connecting with, instructing, and empowering more ladies to assume back command over their funds. This is the way you can join the development:

Be bold

Having every one of the answers is alright not. As a matter of fact, ladies reliably linger behind men in monetary education, and it influences their capacity to go with better monetary choices. That implies ladies feel more scared by money management, retirement arranging, and establishing long-term financial stability. Research shows that 33% of the orientation monetary proficiency hole can be made sense of by ladies' absence of certainty.

Everything no doubt revolves around being bold, and that comes down to certainty. So how would you assemble trust in the monetary world? Attempt these tips:

- Put limited quantities of cash in the financial exchange, so you advance by doing
- Instruct the more youthful age about monetary points early. This is so significant in the event that you have kids!
- Ask your loved ones what they may do

- Request proficient assistance

Discuss cash

As I've referenced beforehand, many individuals are educated from early on to stay away from discussions about cash, and that is particularly valid for ladies. That implies the amount you make, how much your colleagues make, the amount you spend plan... The rundown goes on.

It tends to be truly hard to discuss cash, particularly when there's such a lot of disgrace and mystery encompassing the point. It's not standardized. That is the reason it's so essential to continue shouting out and discussing cash.

At the point when you begin discussing cash with your companions, colleagues, family, and accomplice, you figure out what's conceivable and what's unrealistic. (Did you have any idea that couples that straightforwardly examine their fund's report are far more joyful?) You might learn you're being come up short on, or that you can rethink your financial plan another way. Or on the other hand, perhaps you're reminded to begin zeroing in on saving more. It doesn't need to be off-kilter, and the more we standardize having discussions around cash, the less awkward it will be.

Encircle yourself with positive impacts

You may not feel open to talking with companions or family yet. That is fine. One thing you can do right presently is beginning encircling yourself with positive monetary good examples and monetary teachers, both on the web and disconnected. For instance, virtual entertainment powerhouse Tori Dunlap, the lady behind Her First 100K, offers online counsel to ladies explicitly to assist them with looking into getting themselves in a good position. Another monetary teacher on the web: is Bola Sokunbi of Sharp Young lady Money. Encircling yourself with these voices will assist with normalizing discussing cash, effective financial planning, and creating financial stability.

Shout out working

For countless individuals, the conversations about cash start at work. The more you can advance the circumstance in your own office, the better you make it for all your kindred ladies. In the event that you feel like you're in a situation to make some noise at work, consider upholding things that will assist ladies in your office, as a paid family with leaving, more time off, adaptable working strategies, and the sky is the limit from there.

It additionally implies supporting yourself. Upholding to be paid equivalent to your male partners can be hard to explore. You might try and feel like you have an instance of an inability to embrace success. Yet, truly, haggling at work can have a major effect.

Have your own records

Whether you're hitched or living with your costs combined as one, consider having your own monetary records. You can in any case add to the family costs while dealing with your own cash. Having your own record not just assists with a healthy identity worth, but it can likewise help you in the situation a crisis emerges. Regardless of whether you have major areas of strength, it means quite a bit to keep no less than one record of your own.

Comprehend how you burn through cash

Everybody has their own particular manner of dealing with their funds. Many individuals figure out how to deal with their cash by watching their folks or their companions. Our family story and experience assumes a major part in the way we figure out how to deal with our own funds.

Understanding how you burn through cash can be critical to building a fruitful monetary future. For instance, assuming you realize you overspend on specific costs, you can do whatever it may take to check your propensities or manage them. Knowing your own assets and shortcomings can assist you with better dealing with your cash. Being careful is vital. Toward the month's end, make a point to keep tabs on your development and comprehend how you can get to the next level.

Have individual objectives

Ladies ought to constantly have their own monetary objectives, regardless of their relationship status. Your singular objectives and your objectives with your accomplice can assist you with excelling throughout everyday life, whether that implies taking care of your understudy loans early or saving cash for your kid's future

Cash as a power for good

As far as I might be concerned, cash ought to be a power for good. That implies we ought to send money to put resources into exercises that bring genuine, useful advantages to most individuals, across the world. Simultaneously, we ought not to be putting resources into organizations or areas that carry damage to individuals. Indeed, without a doubt, there is an entire stack of issues and difficulties connected with how we measure benefits or recognize what we mean by hurt. Be that as it may, never do those issues and difficulties mean we ought not to be attempting.

Reasonable financial planning presents a focal point through which we can take a gander at our reality and the individual and cultural objectives we set. At the point when we decide to contribute, when we select a value or an asset, we are going with a decision of one thing over another. We are uncovering our inclination similarly we do as customers when we decide to get one item over another. We are not simply discussing the job of cash. We are discussing the job of organizations and areas, and effectively settling on choices on the ones we need to be champs.

This is no joking matter since, supposing that we acknowledge that we have the capacity to go with informed speculation choices - and we are looking for something past getting more cash - it definitely compels us to scrutinize the motivation behind organizations and the job that they play in the public eye. It's likewise truly enabling us to see the various switches of the progress we have available to us

I most definitely, am fed up with the state of affairs, and being informed ladies can't have an effect. The guidelines of the game can change however almost certainly, we ladies should transform them ourselves.

I really accept that reasonable financial planning presents a chance for ladies like you and me to begin affecting different parts of our aggregate lives. We can instruct and engage ourselves to have an effect on our cash.

The issue is there's not much direction out there for individuals who simply need to get everything rolling on their feasible money management venture. The monetary business doesn't pay a lot of regard to any individual who doesn't have heaps of cash to contribute. Also, that is messed up. The business likewise works really hard at putting individuals off, through crazy language and absurd phrasing. Numerous ladies feel rejected from the monetary business, whether that is a result of certainty, abuse of language that puts us off, or just the manner in which the business collaborates with ladies. The women's activist voice in me is yelling out that this needs to change.

There's another significant pattern as well - we have a heap of information letting us know that numerous ladies are enthusiastic and enlivened by issues of maintainability and that this reaches out to their monetary choices.

The Orientation Contributing Hole

Ladies are not financially planning in a similar way as men, saving less for retirement and stopping more in real money. Furthermore, these outcomes in a huge monetary shortage in the more drawn-out term. Obviously, the orientation pay hole intensifies this shortage, yet it likewise implies that ladies are passing upbringing in the cash they accomplish have turned out better for them. The outcome is that ladies have less abundance and are hoping to resign on substantially less than men.

Keeping your abundance in real money might cause you to have a solid sense of safety; obviously, I grasp that, especially during these violent and testing times. In any case, in the event that you don't begin effectively effective money management of your abundance, you likely could be passing up expected monetary returns.

Simultaneously, you are likewise passing up the chance to accomplish something positive and valuable with it regarding the cultural or natural effect. Assuming you effectively put you can decide to put resources into areas that you truly need to see develop -, for example, clean energy or maintainable customer brands - or proactively put your cash into organizations with solid records on natural and social issues. Anything is possible for you.

So how would you begin?

Manageable financial planning is developing - and that implies that it is becoming simpler for us. Most importantly, focus on what you care about. Ask yourself - what sort of issues mean quite a bit to me? Then make an interpretation of your needs into manageable venture convictions. These are the core values that explain what your identity is and what you need to accomplish with your venture

Then, do some objective setting. What do you maintain that your ventures should achieve? The more unambiguous you are, the simpler it will be to recognize how and where you need to contribute. There is an abundance of data and investigation out there so use it for your potential benefit. Being a reasonable financial backer is tied in with making very much educated, very much thought-about choices.

Conclusion:

Improving ladies ' s cooperation being developed is fundamental for accomplishing civil rights as well as for diminishing neediness. Overall experience shows plainly that supporting a more grounded job for ladies adds to monetary development, further develops youngster endurance and in general family well-being, and diminishes fruitfulness, hence assisting with easing back populace development rates. So, putting resources into ladies is fundamental to a feasible turn of events. But, in spite of these known returns, ladies actually face numerous hindrances in adding to and profiting from advancement. The boundaries start with relatively low interest in female training and wellbeing, they go on with confined admittance to administrations and resources, and they are aggravated by lawful and administrative limitations on ladies ' s open doors. Subsequently, the worldwide progress being developed throughout recent many years has not converted into relative increases for ladies.

Support in pay-creating exercises is of essential interest to ladies all through the creating scene. Ladies take part in those exercises which they feel will bring expanded pay, which they could use to enhance whatever is accessible or gotten by their companions. At times, notwithstanding, the ladies are the providers of the -family.

Ladies likewise contribute enormously to the economies of many emerging nations through food and harvest creation

Ladies included or not associated with pay-creating exercises need credit for the very reasons that men do. One of the principal reasons is to build the family's pay through extended creation and venture and to work on the family's government assistance through expanded utilization. Ladies have been and keep on being vigorously engaged with rustic creation. They need credit to expand their efficiency and -income similarly as rustic advancement plans need to work on ladies' efficiency.